6/15

Just Joking
Joking
Animal Riddles

Get ready for more **LAUGHS!**

NATIONAL
GEOGRAPHIC
KiDS

Just Joking
Animal Riddles

J. Patrick Lewis

Hilarious
riddles, jokes,
and more—
all about
animals!

NATIONAL GEOGRAPHIC
WASHINGTON, D.C.

Did you ever wonder what lice do for fun? **They go on ahead!** And what's another name for well-behaved wildebeests? **Good gnus!**

Dive in to *Just Joking: Animal Riddles*—any page, the front, the back, or in the middle—and you will find funny, punny riddles highlighted by gorgeous photographs of all sorts of wild animals—and some tame ones, too.

HERE'S A RIDDLE ABOUT ME. Can you guess the answer? Unscramble the words **"MARY'S PAINTING,"** and you will learn my favorite two-word insect.

J. Patrick Lewis
Former U.S. Children's Poet Laureate

Here's a hint! Turn to page 208 to check the answer.

4

Q: What am I?

One hundred balls of green and blue just look like eyes behind me, man. I shudder, shake, and turn to you. As birds go, I'm your biggest fan!

A: A PEACOCK

Only the males, called peacocks, have showy tails.

6

I am a
red, blue,
yellow,
and **green**
automatic
answering
machine.

7

Hello?
Hello? Hello?

There are more than 350 different parrot species throughout the world.

Q: What am I ?

These pictures represent parts of a word that make up the name of an animal.

Capybaras are the largest rodents in the world. They can grow to weigh as much as an adult human.

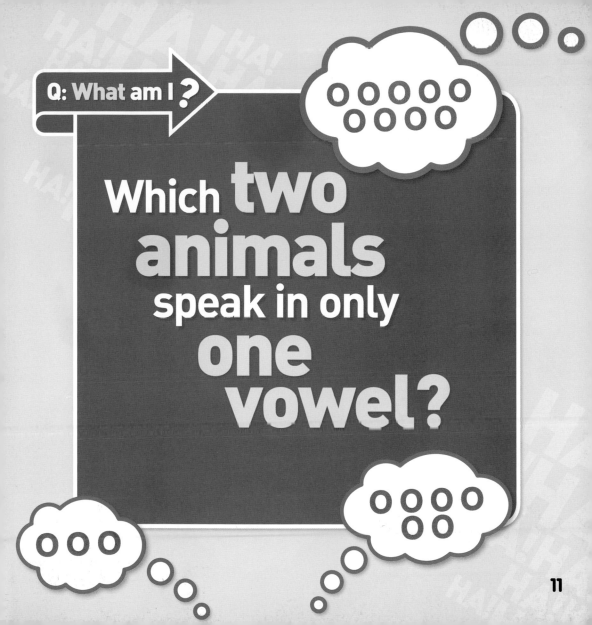

Q: What am I ?

Which **animal** might you find on your **head?**

A: AN EARWIG

Earwigs like to hide out during the day. You might find them in compost, at the base of leaves, or in tree holes.

14

I start with D,

I end with D.

I'm short and small,

I'm long is all.

But no dispute:

I'm doggone cute.

In their native Germany, *dachs* means "badger," and *hund* means "dog." Dachshunds are badger dogs!

What animal keeps on laughing but never gets the joke?

17

What am I?

What **animal** might want an **iPod**, an **iPad**, and an **iPhone?**

Ibex are mountain animals usually living at elevations up to 10,500 feet (3,200 m).

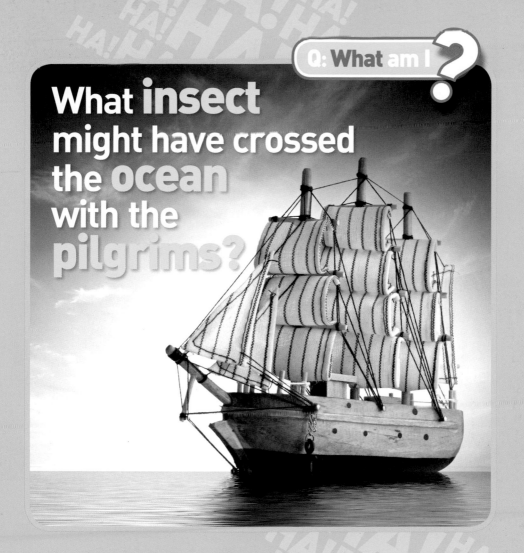

What **insect** might have crossed the **ocean** with the **pilgrims?**

A: A BUTTERFLY ON THE *MAYFLOWER.*

In the middle of a **crocodile**,
behind a **zoo**,
in front of an **ocelot**,
in back of **two**.
Where an **owl** begins,
where a **kangaroo** ends—
that pair in the middle
of the **moon** are friends.

A: THE LETTER *O*.

24

Q **Where can you find a crazy tortoise?**

A In a nutshell.

Tortoises live entirely out of water. So, unlike most turtles, they don't have webbed feet.

Who are you calling crazy?

25

HA! HA! HA!

Q

What do you call a **chicken** crossing the **road?**

A Poultry in motion.

Throne

Hornet. **A**

Raptor

A Parrot.

Sneak

Snake. **A**

27

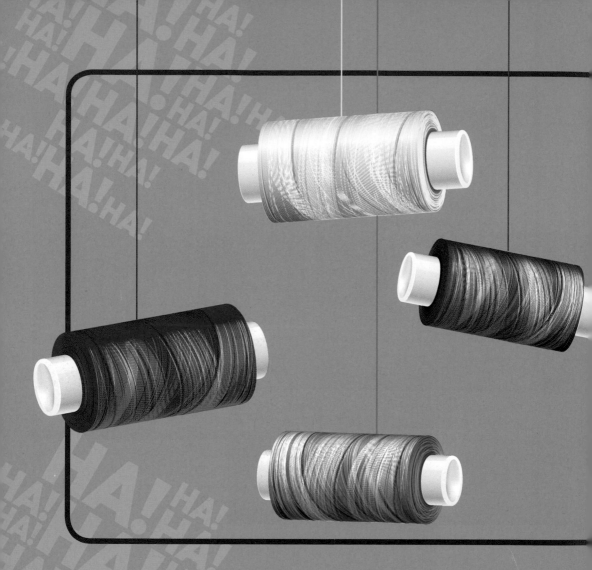

Look me up on the **Internet**.
I hang by a **thread** and
dream all day about
the **World Wide Web**.

Spiders are arachnids, not insects, which means they have eight legs instead of six (like insects).

Q: What am I?

I am a **white beast,**
on **white** land,
hunting for a tasty meal.
For the **big** feast
I have planned,
I'll need an
official seal.

A: A POLAR BEAR

According to myth, polar bears are left-pawed. In fact, they use both equally.

Q: What am I ?

These pictures represent parts of a word
that make up the name of an animal.

A: PORCUPINE

The porcupine is the prickliest of rodents. Their sharp quills lie flat, but when threatened, they leap to attention as a warning to predators.

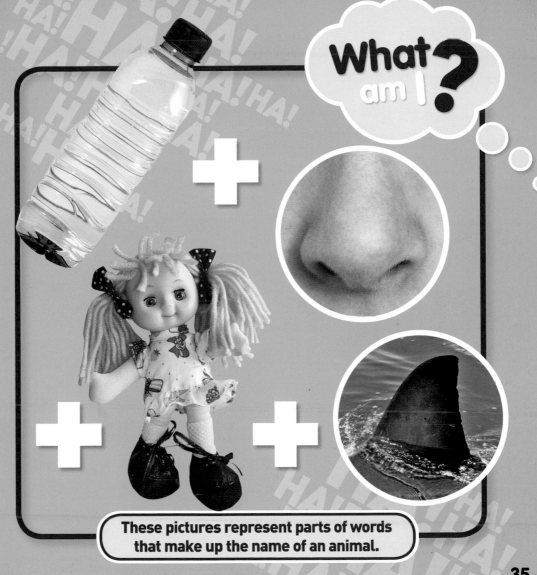

What am I?

These pictures represent parts of words that make up the name of an animal.

BOTTLENOSE DOLPHIN

What kind of **animal** sounds like it lives in a **medicine cabinet?**

Rearrange the letters to make a one-word animal name.

OIL

ORE

A: ORIOLE

The Baltimore oriole is Maryland's official state bird and is even the name of the state's professional baseball team.

What am I?

Inside a **weasel** lives an eel,
inside a **basset hound**, a bat,
inside an **antelope**, an ape,
inside a **rabbit** lives a rat,
inside a **chicken** lives a hen,
inside a **beaver** lives a bear,
inside a **mongoose** lives a moose,
inside a **marmoset**,
a _ _ _ _ _.

Some animal names have 6 letters, and some have 10 letters. Which animal names have 2 letters?

A:

All animals' names have (at least) 2 letters.

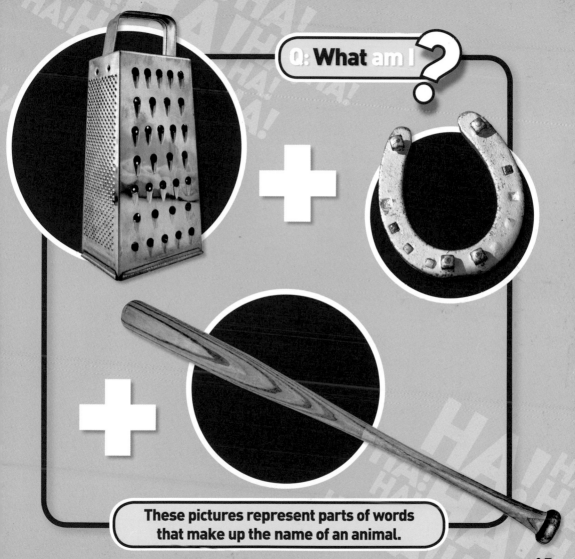

Q: What am I ?

These pictures represent parts of words that make up the name of an animal.

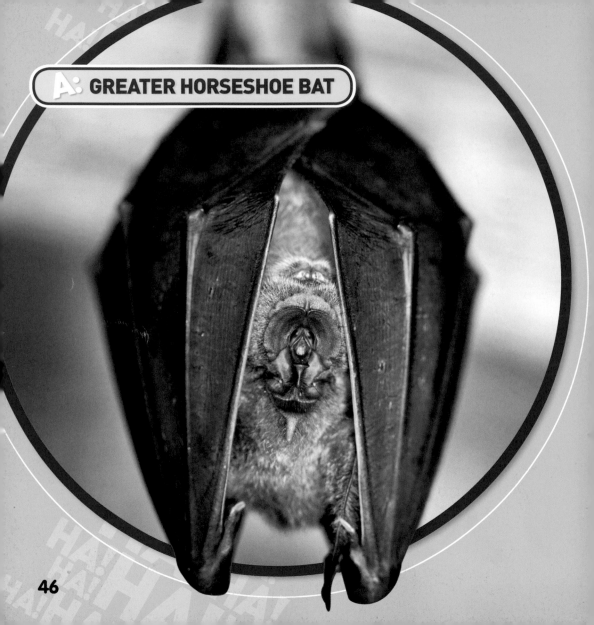

A: GREATER HORSESHOE BAT

These pictures represent parts of a word that make up the name of an animal.

SQUIRRELS

Q The difference between a **dock** and a **duck** is the difference between a **back** and a **buck** is the difference between a **bag** and a **bug** is the difference between a **pig** and a **pug.**

A The letter U.

49

Q

There was a pug from
Whited,
Who had become
excited
Because he'd been
invited
To see a baseball game.
When everyone was
seated,
The pug was warmly
greeted.
Three letters I've **repeated**
Six times.
What is his name?

A

Ted.

Pugs, toy dogs with wrinkly faces, were bred almost 3,000 years ago and were pets of Buddhist monks in Tibet.

50

Shore

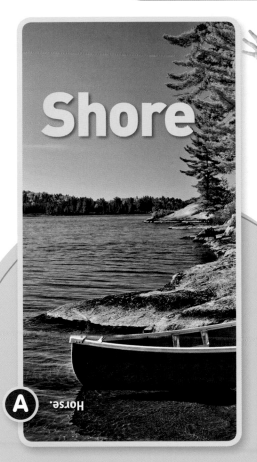

Horse.

A

Paroled

Leopard.

A

Pea

Ape.

A

51

½ of a **target**

²⁄₃ of an **ant**

HA!HA!HA!

52

What am I?

⅓ of a **turtle**

½ of a **lamb**

53

TARANTULA

Despite their scary appearance, spiders rarely bite people.

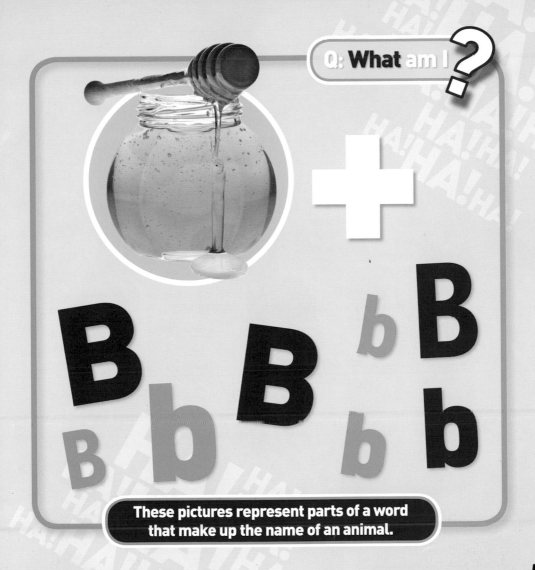

Q: **What am I?**

These pictures represent parts of a word
that make up the name of an animal.

55

A: HONEYBEES

In **between** the  and  see if you can spot the **animal** with the world's most gigantic **pot!**

A: A HIPPOPOTAMUS

A hippopotamus (meaning "river horse") is the third largest land mammal after the elephant and the white rhino.

What am I?

Poor pies

Rearrange the letters to make a one-word animal name.

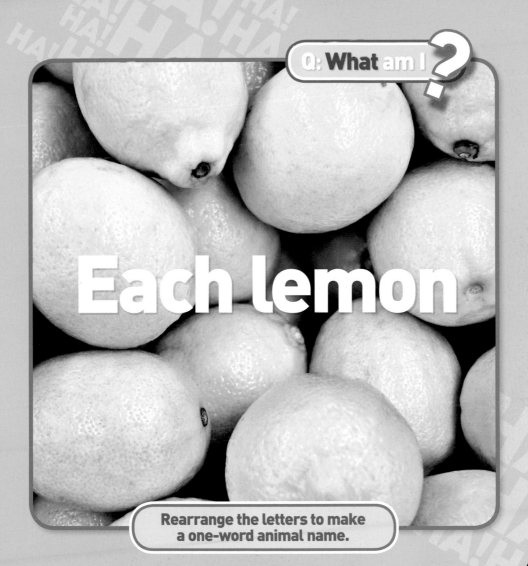

Q: What am I?

Each lemon

Rearrange the letters to make a one-word animal name.

Suppose you see a **bunch of animals racing** across the **grasslands.** Which one will probably **win** by a **neck?**

65

A: A GIRAFFE

A giraffe can clean its ears with its tongue!

What am I?

Smug ant

Rearrange the letters to make a one-word animal name.

67

One of **eight**
(a special herd),
who thinks that
he's a **winter bird**
without **feathers**,
only **hoofs**,
which he thumps
on lots of **roofs**.

What **letter** must be added to **"new"** to make an **aquatic amphibian,** also known as **an eft?**

71

A: THE LETTER *T*—NEWT

A newt can grow new limbs, eye lenses, spinal cord, and part of its heart.

HA! HA! HA!

Q **What's a purrfect cat car?**

A A jaguar.

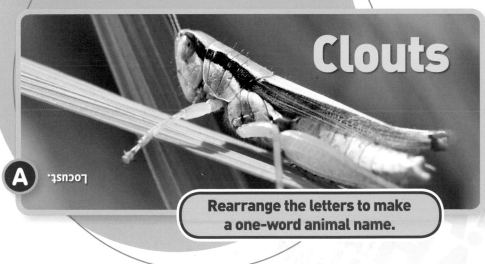

Clouts

A Locust.

Rearrange the letters to make a one-word animal name.

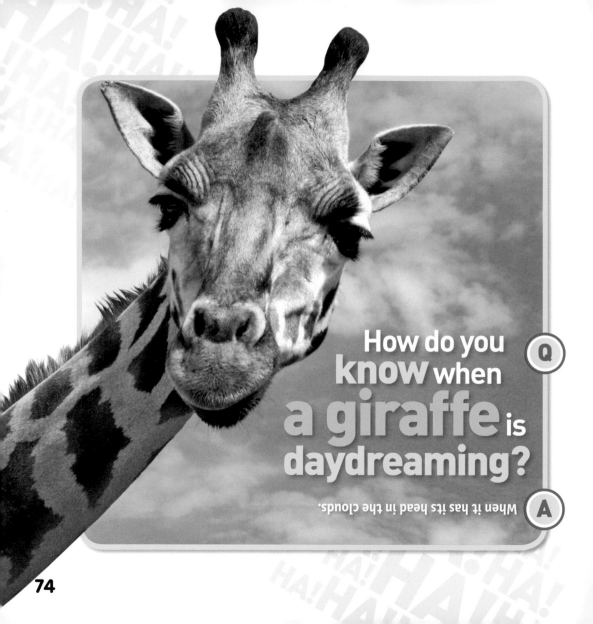

How do you **know** when **a giraffe** is **daydreaming?** **Q**

When it has its head in the clouds. **A**

Q Which letter plus which number spells "dog"?

A K + 9 = Canine.

Q How do you draw great safari pictures?

A Try to stay outside the lions.

Faster than a **stone** can **sink,** faster than an **eye** can **blink,** this **river animal** is often mistaken for a **mink!**

River otters are large and muscular, with broad heads. Minks are small and slender, with pointed snouts.

Q: What am I?

SNORE

CHOIR

Rearrange the letters to make a one-word animal name.

A: RHINOCEROS

Some goon

Rearrange the letters to make
a one-word animal name.

81

MONGOOSE

The mongoose is famous for boldly attacking deadly snakes like the cobra.

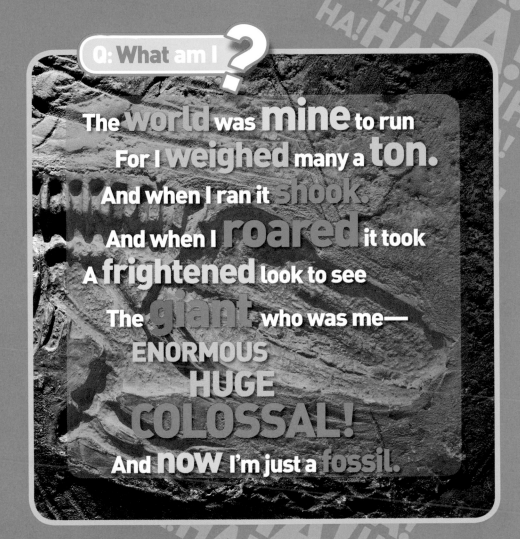

Q: What am I?

The world was mine to run
For I weighed many a ton.
And when I ran it shook.
And when I roared it took
A frightened look to see

The giant who was me—
ENORMOUS
HUGE
COLOSSAL!
And now I'm just a fossil.

A: A DINOSAUR

Many dinosaurs were vegetarians, despite their vicious reputations.

Meek rat

Rearrange the letters to make
a one-word animal name.

What am I?

How many **birds** are lighter than a **feather**? Not any. But this **tiny** flier weighs **less** than a **penny.**

87

Hummingbirds can flap their wings 50 to 200 times per second.

A **South American animal** that you would come across **a lot** is like a little **leopard** known to science as an _____.

89

A: OCELOT

"Ocelot" comes from the Mexican Aztec word meaning "field tiger."

What am I?

If you are not a **Labrador retriever** or a **poodle,** you might be something in between we call a

_ _ _ _ _ _ _ _ _ _ _ _ .

LABRADOODLE

The Labradoodle was introduced in 1988 when an Australian breeder crossed a Labrador retriever and standard poodle to create a new guide dog for the blind.

She **laughs** more than anyone among the **grassland** folk. Amazing, since she doesn't even have to hear a **joke.**

What am I?

Beginning in late
May or June,

its droning drowns
the afternoon
with rhythms from
a thousand wings.
It's like a symphony of strings,
whose tiny violinists crawl
all around this music hall,
which has a door and
has a dome,
and really is their
home sweet home.

A
BEEHIVE

In July and August, the height of bee season, a typical beehive can have as many as 80,000 honeybees.

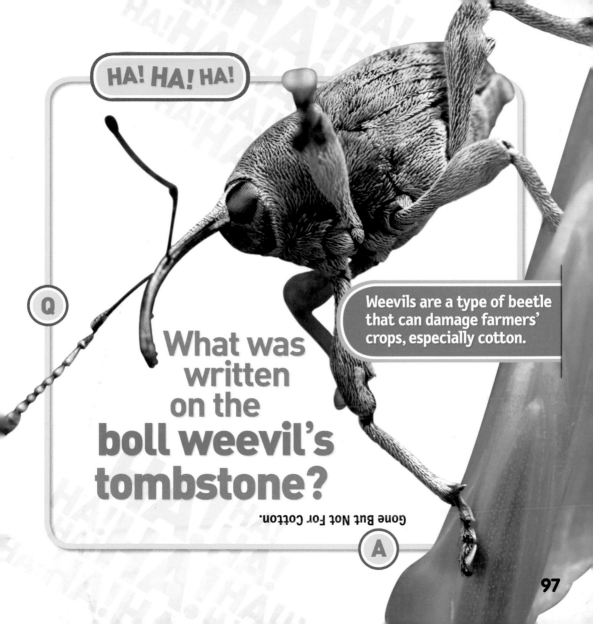

HA! HA! HA!

Q

What was
written
on the
**boll weevil's
tombstone?**

Weevils are a type of beetle
that can damage farmers'
crops, especially cotton.

Gone But Not For Cotton.

A

97

Q What happened when the fisherman was about to take a worm off the hook?

A He debated.

Q Does an iguana ever hang out with a lizard?

A Only if the iguana wanna.

98

Q What do you call a green dog?

A A broc-collie.

Q What do you get when you cross a hamster with a buffalo?

A A gerbull.

Q What makes **poplar** and **aspen trees** shake so much?

A Eager beavers.

Q: What am I?

What kind of **dog** has **bad manners?**

A: A POINTER

One of the oldest breed of sporting dog, pointers trace back more than 300 years.

Q: What am I?

There's one **insect** **everyone** knows **that** meets its **mate** and leaves it **dead.** It's also the **one** and **only insect** that can **swivel** its **head.**

A: A PRAYING MANTIS

+

E

These pictures represent parts of a word
that make up the name of an animal.

MONKEY

+

These pictures represent parts of a word
that make up the name of an animal.

107

Q: What am I ?

These pictures represent parts of a word that make up the name of an animal.

A: MANATEE

110

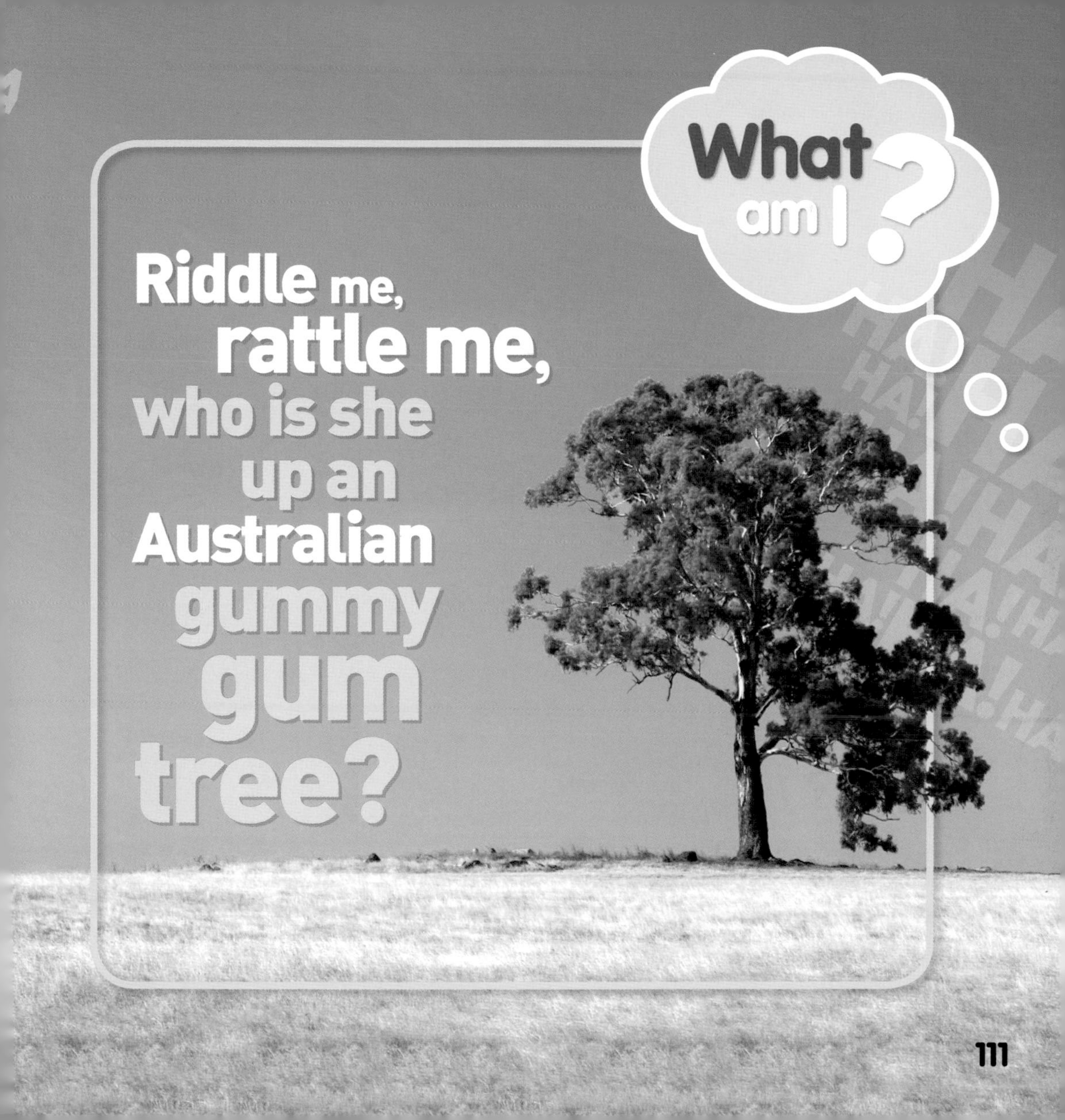

Riddle me,
rattle me,
who is she
up an
Australian
gummy
gum
tree?

A KOALA

Native to Australia, a koala eats eucalyptus leaves and almost nothing else.

I am **dull** as dirt.
Watch out, I'll
eat your **shirt!**
My **cousin's** not so naughty:
A **butterfly's** a hottie.
Who am I?

Q: What am I?

A mall

Rearrange the letters to make a one-word animal name.

What am I?

Twirl changer

Rearrange the letters to make
a two-word animal name.

117

NIGHT CRAWLER

Riddle me, rattle me, who's the **cat** orange and **black** and **striped** like that?

Tigers are the
largest cat species.

HA! HA! HA!

Q: What do you call the area where worms live?

A: The robin 'hood.

Q: What does a trucker call an armadillo?

A: A speed bump.

121

Q What's **in** a **cat** but **gone** in a **dog**? What's **in** a **toad**, but **not** in a **frog**? What's **in** a **boar** but **lost** in a **hog**?

A The letter A.

122

Q What do you call a tree with a French owl sitting in it?

A The Eyeful Tower.

Q What's another name for well-behaved wildebeests?

A Good gnus.

123

+

These pictures represent parts of a word
that make up the name of an animal.

124

I start with **P**,
I end with **A.**
AND I connect
them in my
own way.

Though scientists hope to increase their numbers, giant pandas are on the brink of extinction, with only about 1,600 left in the wild.

+

These pictures represent parts of words
that make up the name of an animal.

129

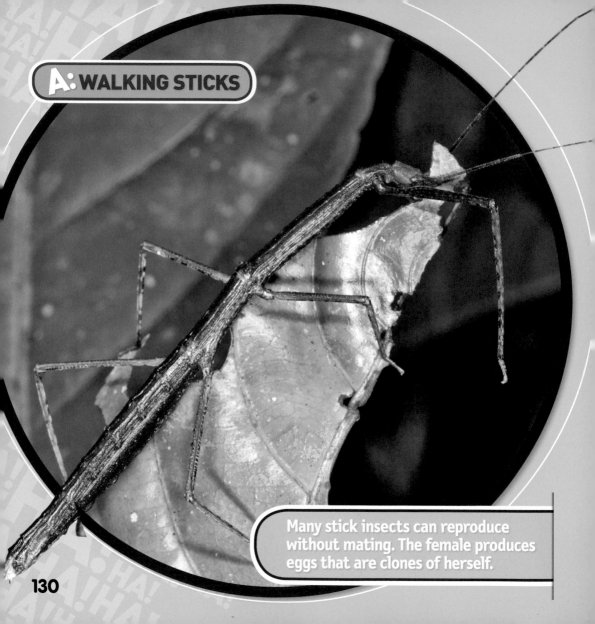

A: WALKING STICKS

Many stick insects can reproduce without mating. The female produces eggs that are clones of herself.

Which **invertebrate** has a **unit of measurement** in its name?

What am I?

HA! HA! HA! HA! HA! HA! HA! HA!

What
takes off
its **coat**
and **pants**
when it's **hot?**

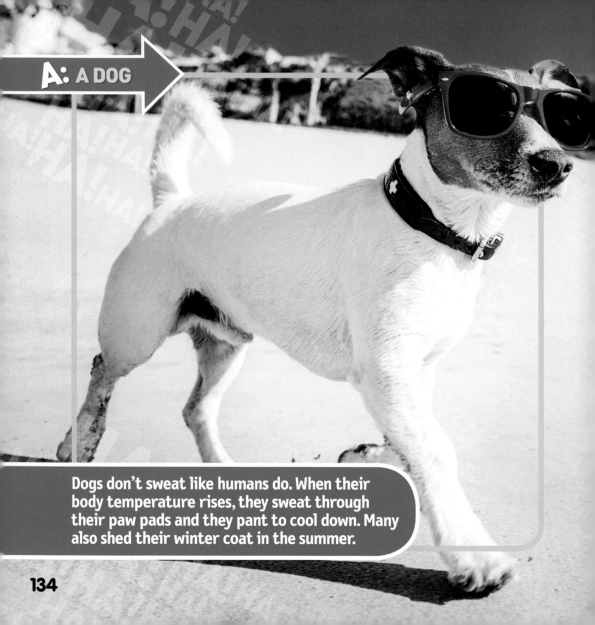

Dogs don't sweat like humans do. When their body temperature rises, they sweat through their paw pads and they pant to cool down. Many also shed their winter coat in the summer.

This **anti-mule**
is, as a rule,
impossible
to push or pull.

135

A: A DONKEY

Donkeys are stronger than horses of the same size.

What am I?

Ccan yyou gguess

ttwo aanimals

wwhose **nnames**

bbegin wwith

iidentical lletters?

A LLAMA AND AN AARDVARK

An aardvark can eat 50,000 termites each night.

138

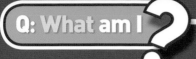
I sing a single **syllable of wind,** the music of the trees in **moonlit woods.** My eyes are fixed on headlight **night patrol** for **rodent thieves** in **rodent neighborhoods.**

Who are you calling a thief?

A: AN OWL

Though owls tend to be loners, a group of owls is called a parliament.

He's **not** exactly **orange.**
There is a **big dispute**
about this **brownish-reddish**
Borneo galoot.
He **isn't** really **pink,**
and you can see he's **not.**
He looks like he's
orangutapricot.

Orangutans are sometimes called "red apes," though their name really means "person of the forest" in the Malay language.

142

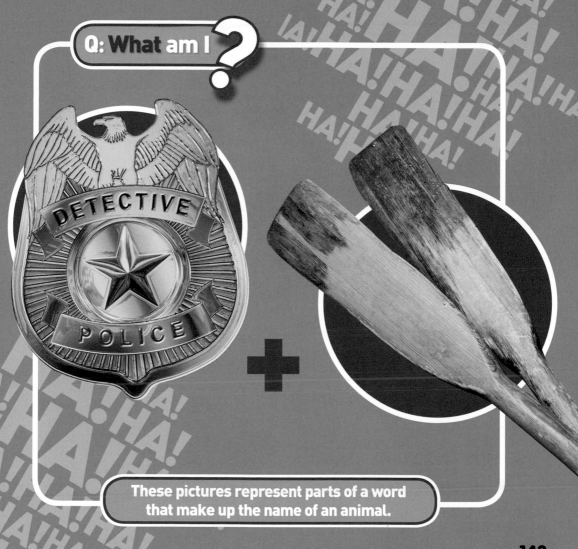

Q: What am I ?

DETECTIVE POLICE

+

These pictures represent parts of a word that make up the name of an animal.

143

Q Where can you **always** find the **rare quagga?**

A In the dictionary.

Q Name the fastest bird in the world without using the words "golden eagle."

A Peregrine falcon.

145

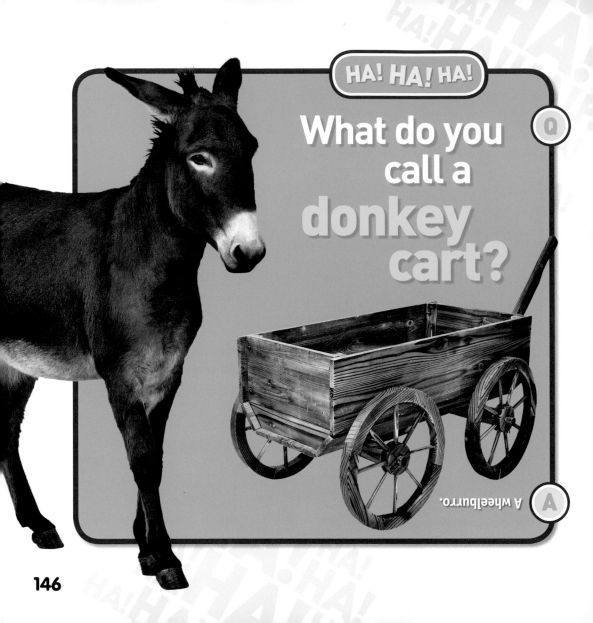

HA! HA! HA!

What do you call a donkey cart? Q

A wheelburro. A

146

Q What's the difference between a gnu and a wildebeest?

A Only the spelling—the animals are the same.

Q The *three-toed sloth* has three toes on four feet. So the *three-toed sloth* has twelve toes. The *two-toed sloth* has two toes on its front feet and three toes on its hind feet. How many toes do two *two-toed sloths* have? Ten? Try again!

A A two-toed sloth has ten toes. Two two-toed sloths would have twenty toes.

147

Two letters describe
One **big** dude,
In a very bad mood.

148

This **huff-and-puffer** **pulls a** plow So far, you'll be shouting, "Holy Cow!"

149

A: AN OX

Oxen can pull heavier loads for a longer period of time than horses, although they are slower!

I have **five letters** in my **name**, and **three** of them are the **same.** **1, 3,** and **4** (that's an extra clue). I know what I'm called. **Do you?**

Q: What am I ?

+ **er** +

These pictures represent parts of a word that make up the name of an animal.

153

Down in the **deep,** there lives an odd **battery-powered** lightning rod. What is it?

A: AN ELECTRIC EEL

The electricity of an electric eel is about five times more powerful than a U.S. wall socket.

What am I?

I am a **helmet**
on the ground
but so afraid
of strangers,
I disappear,
inside my **hat**.
The world is full
of dangers.

157

A TURTLE

Turtles have been around for more than 200 million years.

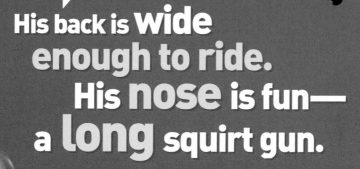

His back is **wide** enough to ride. His **nose** is fun— a **long** squirt gun.

His **ears**, perhaps, are **giant** flaps. The teeth you see, are **ivory**.

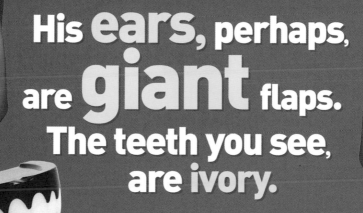

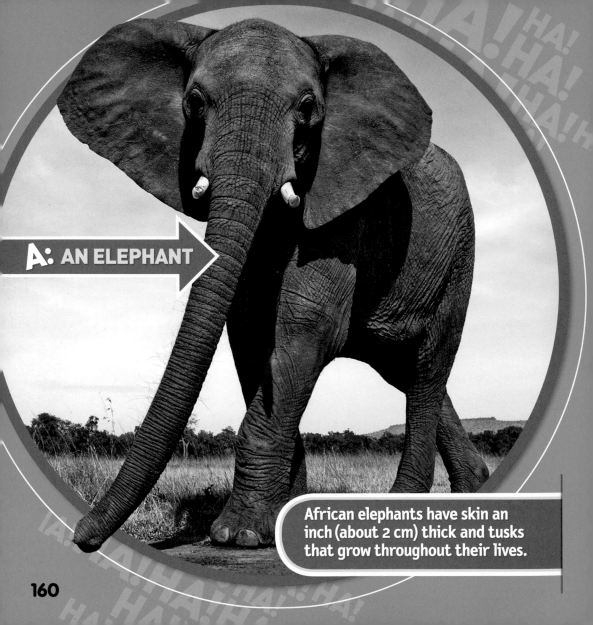

A: AN ELEPHANT

African elephants have skin an inch (about 2 cm) thick and tusks that grow throughout their lives.

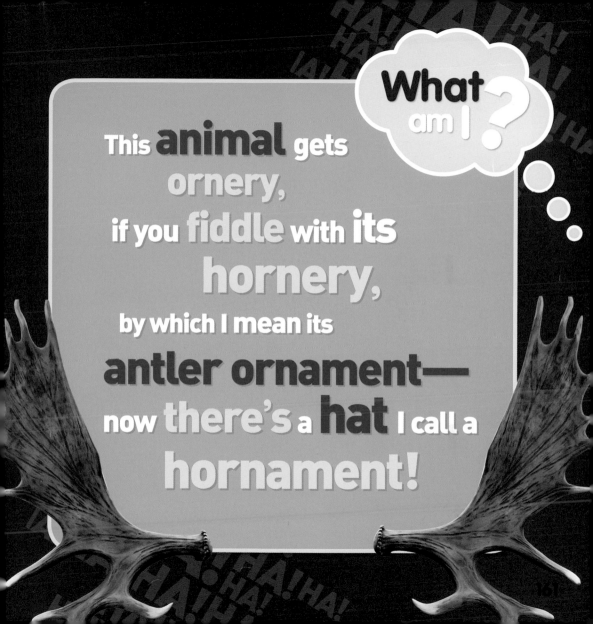

Only a male (or bull) moose has antlers, which it sheds every winter and grows back in the spring.

She's **first** in line
to **redesign**
a **ball** of **twine**
into a **mess.**

But she **adapts**
nicely to **naps**
in **people's laps**—
the **Em-purr-ess.**

A: A CAT

Cats are America's most popular pet: 95 million cats to 83 million dogs.

Q: What am I?

What **bird** appears at every **dinner?**

A: A SWALLOW

Did someone say dinner? Mmm ...

Barn swallows build cup-shaped nests out of mud.

What am I?

These pictures represent parts of words that make up an animal phrase.

Q

How are **dogs** like **coins?**

They both have heads and tails.

A

169

Q What does a yak have to look forward to every morning?

A A bad hair day.

Q Of all the **continents**, **Antarctica's** the one to break the record for **not** having a single _ _ _ _ _.

A Snake.

170

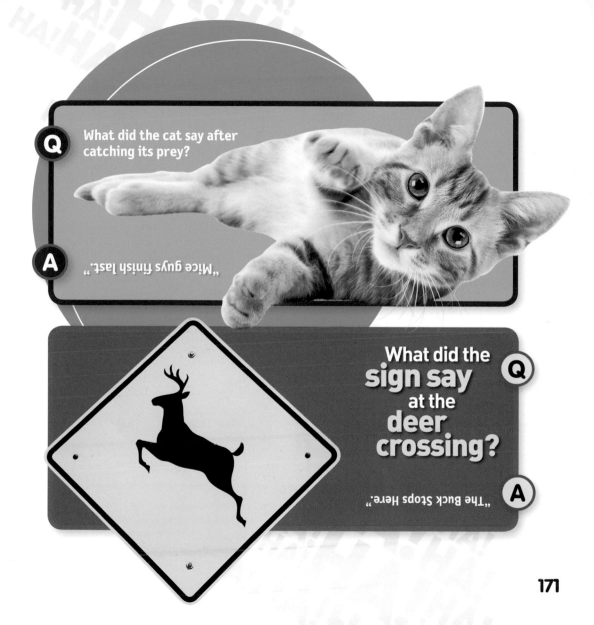

Q What did the cat say after catching its prey?

A "Mice guys finish last."

Q What did the **sign say** at the **deer crossing?**

A "The Buck Stops Here."

171

Q

In the woods a pesky critter
Makes hikers reconsider:
Pull your socks and
shorts up quick
If you feel a
burrowing: _ _ _ _!

A Tick.

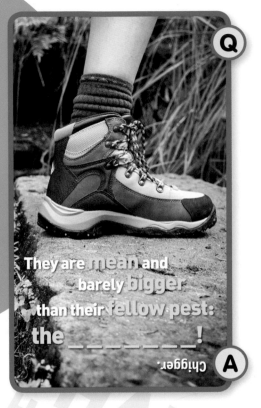

Q

They are mean and
barely bigger
than their fellow pest:
the _ _ _ _ _ _ _!

A Chigger.

Chiggers and ticks are not insects but arachnids (like spiders). Warm, soapy water will wash chiggers off your skin. Ticks must be removed gently with tweezers and can be saved in rubbing alcohol for disease diagnosis. Ticks love dogs and cats, so it is important to keep your household pets free of them.

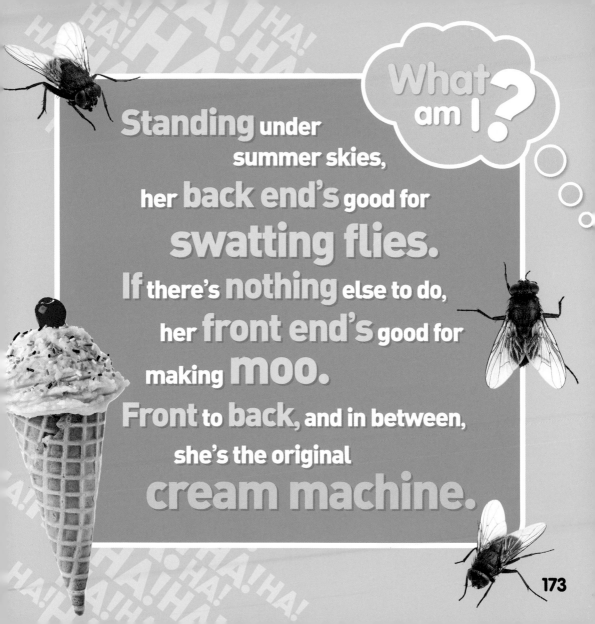

What am I?

Standing under summer skies, her **back end's** good for **swatting flies.** If there's **nothing** else to do, her **front end's** good for making **moo.** Front to **back,** and in between, she's the original **cream machine.**

173

Flamingos
all along the **Nile**
put a **smile** on the

_ _ _ _ _ _ _ _ _ _ _ _ _ _ .

A: CROCODILE

Like turtles, crocodiles are cold-blooded reptiles, and they have the strongest bite of any animal in the world.

176

She doesn't **give milk,** cream, butter, or **cheese.**
She's not equipped to give any of these.
What she will give you, of all sorts, is lots and lots and lots and lots of **snorts.**

177

A PIG

There are about one billion pigs in the world.

1 foot to **thump,**
2 feet to **sit,**
4 feet to **jump,**
lickety-split!

179

Q: What am I?

Spring wings into the backyard ready to play tug-a-worm.

A: A ROBIN

These pictures represent parts of a word that make up the name of an animal.

168

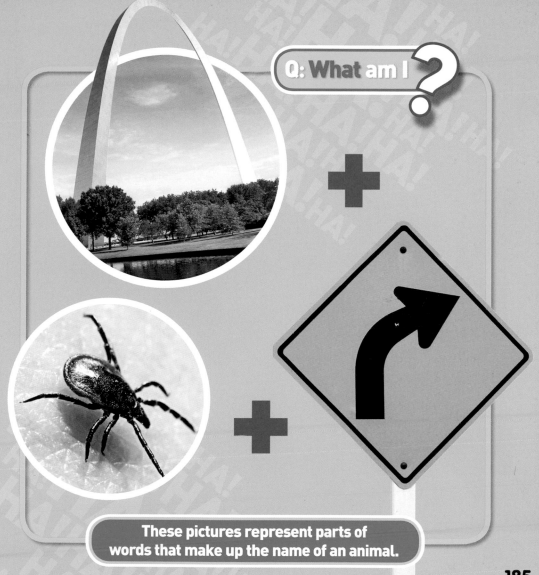

Q: What am I ?

These pictures represent parts of words that make up the name of an animal.

Her **nose** drills **hills** where there's a chance **ants** will **stick** to sprung **tongue** and become **dinner** in her!

What am I?

Giant anteaters have no teeth but their tongues are long enough to capture 35,000 insects at a time.

Q Can you **change a wasp into a fish** by **changing one letter** in wasp **three times?**

Wasp
Wash
Wish
Fish

Though **bugs** may live **high** in the **trees**,

underground or in stagnant **water**,

under **rugs**, outside in gardens,

in **climates** **hot** and **hotter**,

this **bug** believes life is **greater** **under a refrigerator!**

A: A COCKROACH

Most cockroaches can live for several weeks without food and a week without water, and large species can even live headless for a week!

HA! HA! HA!

Q Where did the narwhal get his long horn?

A That's beside the point.

Q What did the mole say to the earthworm?

A "What rock did you crawl out from under?"

Q Why did the blue jay want a computer?

A To tweet on Twitter.

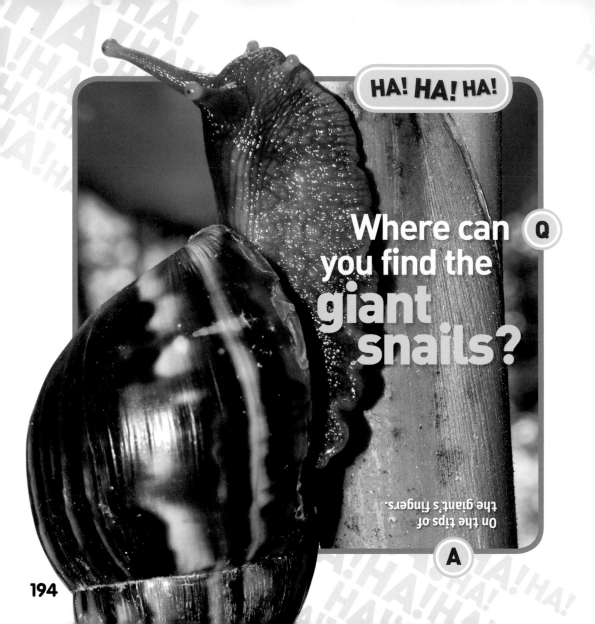

Where can you find the giant snails? Q

On the tips of the giant's fingers.

A

DONKEY 1:
Did you enjoy playing tug-of-war?

DONKEY 2:
Yes, I got a kick out of it.

Q What do lice do for fun?

A They go on ahead.

My **little** friends and I love **wood.** Your **houses** made of **wood** are good. Our **houses** look like **towers** for **giant colonies** of ours, like this one! It's the perfect **nest—** a miniature **Mound** Everest.

A: A TERMITE

Among the world's greatest laborers, termites work 24/7—they never sleep.

Q: **What am I** ?

+ **E**

+

These pictures represent parts of words
that make up the name of an animal.

A: BALD EAGLE

200

Bald eagles can live up
to 28 years in the wild.

Now **that** was funny!

JOKEFINDER

JOKEFINDER

ILLUSTRATION CREDITS

To Olivia and Ben
—JPL

Staff for This Book
Shelby Alinsky, *Project Editor*
Julide Obuz Dengel, *Art Director*
Lisa Jewell, Vanessa Mack *Photo Editors*
Bri Bertoia, *Special Projects Assistant*
Erica Holsclaw, *Special Projects Assistant*
Allie Allen, *Design Production Assistant*
Margaret Leist, *Photo Assistant*
Grace Hill, *Associate Managing Editor*
Joan Gossett, *Production Editor*
Lewis R. Bassford, *Production Manager*
Rachel Faulise, *Manager, Production Services*
Susan Borke, *Legal and Business Affairs*

Design by Plan B Book Packagers

Published by the National Geographic Society
Gary E. Knell, *President and CEO*
John M. Fahey, Jr., *Chairman of the Board*
Declan Moore, *Chief Media Officer*
Melina Gerosa Bellows, *Chief Education Officer*
Hector Sierra, *Senior Vice President and General Manager, Book Division*

Senior Management Team, Kids Publishing and Media
Nancy Laties Feresten, *Senior Vice President;* Jennifer Emmett, *Vice President, Editorial Director, Kids Books;* Julie Vosburgh Agnone, *Vice President, Editorial Operations;* Rachel Buchholz, *Editor and Vice President,* NG Kids *magazine;* Michelle Sullivan, *Vice President, Kids Digital;* Eva Absher-Schantz, *Design Director;* Jay Sumner, *Photo Director;* Hannah August, *Marketing Director;* R. Gary Colbert, *Production Director*

Digital
Anne McCormack, *Director;* Laura Goertzel, Sara Zeglin, *Producers;* Jed Winer, *Special Projects Assistant;* Emma Rigney, *Creative Producer;* Brian Ford, *Video Producer;* Bianca Bowman, *Assistant Producer;* Natalie Jones, *Senior Product Manager*

The National Geographic Society is one of the world's largest nonprofit scientific and educational organizations. Founded in 1888 to "increase and diffuse geographic knowledge," the Society's mission is to inspire people to care about the planet. It reaches more than 400 million people worldwide each month through its official journal, *National Geographic*, and other magazines; National Geographic Channel; television documentaries; music; radio; films; books; DVDs; maps; exhibitions; live events; school publishing programs; interactive media; and merchandise. National Geographic has funded more than 10,000 scientific research, conservation, and exploration projects and supports an education program promoting geographic literacy.

For more information, please visit nationalgeographic.com,
call 1-800-NGS LINE (647-5463), or write to the following address:
National Geographic Society
1145 17th Street N.W.
Washington, D.C. 20036-4688 U.S.A.

Visit us online at nationalgeographic.com/books

For librarians and teachers: ngchildrensbooks.org

More for kids from National Geographic: kids.nationalgeographic.com

For information about special discounts for bulk purchases, please contact National Geographic Books Special Sales: ngspecsales@ngs.org

For rights or permissions inquiries, please contact National Geographic Books Subsidiary Rights: ngbookrights@ngs.org

Paperback ISBN: 978-1-4263-1869-6
Reinforced Library Binding ISBN: 978-1-4263-1870-2

Printed in China

14/PPS/1

Answer to riddle on page 4: praying mantis